CHI

DK READERS

Level 3

Spacebusters: The Race to the Moon
Beastly Tales
Shark Attack!
Titanic
Invaders from Outer Space
Movie Magic
Plants Bite Back!
Time Traveler
Bermuda Triangle
Tiger Tales
Aladdin
Heidi
Zeppelin: The Age of the Airship
Spies
Terror on the Amazon
Disasters at Sea
The Story of Anne Frank
Abraham Lincoln: Lawyer, Leader, Legend
George Washington: Soldier, Hero, President
Extreme Sports
Spiders' Secrets

The Big Dinosaur Dig
Space Heroes: Amazing Astronauts
The Story of Chocolate
School Days Around the World
LEGO: Mission to the Arctic
NFL: Super Bowl Heroes
NFL: Peyton Manning
NFL: Whiz Kid Quarterbacks
MLB: Home Run Heroes: Big Mac, Sammy, and Junior
MLB: Roberto Clemente
MLB: Roberto Clemente *en español*
MLB: World Series Heroes
MLB: Record Breakers
MLB: Down to the Wire: Baseball's Great Pennant Races
Star Wars: Star Pilot
The X-Men School
Abraham Lincoln: Abogado, Líder, Leyenda *en español*
Al Espacio: La Carrera a la Luna *en español*

Level 4

Days of the Knights
Volcanoes and Other Natural Disasters
Secrets of the Mummies
Pirates! Raiders of the High Seas
Horse Heroes
Trojan Horse
Micro Monsters
Going for Gold!
Extreme Machines
Flying Ace: The Story of Amelia Earhart
Robin Hood
Black Beauty
Free at Last! The Story of Martin Luther King, Jr.
Joan of Arc
Spooky Spinechillers
Welcome to The Globe! The Story of Shakespeare's Theater
Antarctic Adventure
Space Station: Accident on Mir
Atlantis: The Lost City?
Dinosaur Detectives
Danger on the Mountain: Scaling the World's Highest Peaks
Crime Busters
The Story of Muhammad Ali
First Flight: The Story of the Wright Brothers
D-Day Landings: the Story of the Allied Invasion
Solo Sailing
LEGO: Race for Survival
NFL: NFL's Greatest Upsets

NFL: Rumbling Running Backs
NFL: Super Bowl!
MLB: Strikeout Kings
MLB: Super Shortstops: Jeter, Nomar, and A-Rod
MLB: The Story of the New York Yankees
MLB: The World of Baseball
MLB: October Magic: All the Best World Series!
WCW: Feel the Sting
WCW: Going for Goldberg
JLA: Batman's Guide to Crime and Detection
JLA: Superman's Guide to the Universe
JLA: Aquaman's Guide to the Oceans
JLA: Wonder Woman's Book of Myths
JLA: Flash's Guide to Speed
JLA: Green Lantern's Guide to Great Inventions
The Story of the X-Men: How it all Began
Creating the X-Men: How Comic Books Come to Life
Spider-Man's Amazing Powers
The Story of Spider-Man
The Incredible Hulk's Book of Strength
The Story of the Incredible Hulk
Transformers: The Awakening
Transformers: The Quest
Transformers: The Unicron Battles
Transformers: The Uprising
Transformers: Megatron Returns
Transformers: Terracon Attack
Star Wars: Galactic Crisis!

A Note to Parents

DK READERS is a compelling program for beginning readers, designed in conjunction with leading literacy experts, including Dr. Linda Gambrell, Professor of Education at Clemson University. Dr. Gambrell has served as President of the National Reading Conference and the College Reading Association, and has recently been elected to serve as President of the International Reading Association.

Beautiful illustrations and superb full-color photographs combine with engaging, easy-to-read stories to offer a fresh approach to each subject in the series. Each DK READER is guaranteed to capture a child's interest while developing his or her reading skills, general knowledge, and love of reading.

The five levels of DK READERS are aimed at different reading abilities, enabling you to choose the books that are exactly right for your child:

Pre-level 1: Learning to read
Level 1: Beginning to read
Level 2: Beginning to read alone
Level 3: Reading alone
Level 4: Proficient readers

The "normal" age at which a child begins to read can be anywhere from three to eight years old. Adult participation through the lower levels is very helpful for providing encouragement, discussing storylines, and sounding out unfamiliar words.

No matter which level you select, you can be sure that you are helping your child learn to read, then read to learn!

LONDON, NEW YORK, MUNICH,
MELBOURNE, and DELHI

Series Editor Deborah Lock
Senior Art Editor Sonia Moore
Art Editor Sadie Thomas
U.S. Editor John Searcy
DTP Designer Emma Hansen-Knarhoi
Production Georgina Hayworth
Picture Researcher Myriam Megharbi
Jacket Designer Sonia Moore
Reading Consultant
Linda Gambrell, Ph.D.

First American Edition, 2007
07 08 09 10 11 10 9 8 7 6 5 4 3 2 1
Published in the United States by DK Publishing
375 Hudson Street, New York, New York 10014

Published in Great Britain by Dorling Kindersley Limited

DK books are available at special discounts when purchased in bulk
for sales promotions, premiums, fund-raising, or educational use.
For details, contact:
DK Publishing Special Markets
375 Hudson Street
New York, NY 10014
SpecialSales@dk.com

A catalog record for this book is available
from the Library of Congress.
ISBN: 978-0-7566-2548-1 (Paperback)
ISBN: 978-0-7566-2549-8 (Hardcover)

Color reproduction by Colourscan, Singapore
Printed and bound in China by L Rex Printing Co., Ltd.

The publisher would like to thank the following for their kind
permission to reproduce their photographs:
(Key: a=above; b=below/bottom; c=center; l=left; r=right; t=top)
Alamy Images: Juniors Bildarchiv 17bl; Nick Cobbing 27br; Digital
Archive Japan 5cra, 13b, 15b, 16c, 17b; Garry Gay 14cl; Greenshoots
Communications 24-25b, 25cra, 26tr, 27c, 28-29, 29br; Image100 17br;
Luke Peters 47tr; Photo Japan 14tr; Dan White 5cb, 18-19, 20b, 22t, 23tr,
23br, 23clb, 23cla. **Corbis:** The Art Archive 40crb; Will & Deni McIntyre
37br; Vince Streano 12cl; TWPhoto 15tr; Michael S. Yamashita 17tr.
Getty Images: The Image Bank/Angelo Cavalli 43br; The Image Bank/
John William Banagan 9cla; The Image Bank/Theo Allofs 9cl; Stone/Paul
Chesley 13tr; Stone+/Ludger 17bc; Taxi/Chris Clinton 33br. **The Hindu
Photo Archives:** Kasturi and Sons Ltd/K R Deepak 21t; Kasturi and Sons
Ltd/M Vedhan 21cr. **Jeremy Mates/sial.org:** 46tl; **Max Moore:** 21b.

With thanks to: Solomon and his class at Annandale Public School
arranged by Miranda Kitchenside-Quinn, photographed by Cath Muscat;
Francis and his class at Coldfall Primary School arranged by Karen
Robinson, photographed by Simon Rawles; Samantha and her class at
C.A.Dwyer Elementary School arranged by Mindy Klarman and
photographed by David Mager of Pearson Learning Group; Frida in Peru
was based on CAFOD's story photographed by Simon Rawles.
All other images © Dorling Kindersley Limited
For more information see: www.dkimages.com

Discover more at
www.dk.com

Contents

 **READERS**

READING
3
ALONE

School Days
Around the World

Written by Catherine Chambers

DK Publishing

Meet the children

All around the world, children go to school. In this book, seven children will show you what it's like to go to school in their countries.

Samantha from Wharton, New Jersey, USA

They are all celebrating World Earth Day, a day set aside for valuing the natural world.

Frida from Santo Tomas, Peru

They all live in very different environments but many things about their school days are similar. They all play games and they all do math!

Francis from London, England

Riku from Tokyo, Japan

Aseye [A-say-yay] from Accra, Ghana [GAH-na]

Solomon from Sydney, New South Wales, Australia

Rupa from Andhra Pradesh [AHN-druh pruh-DAESH], India

Now turn the page to begin your around-the-world school adventure! ❖

Solomon in Australia

Hi folks. It's Solomon here in Australia. I was in a bit of a rush this morning and nearly forgot the spinifex grass I needed for our Earth Day project.

I yanked on my school sweatshirt, grabbed my bag, and pulled on my sun hat—all at the same time.

"Where's your spinifex, Solomon?" asked Mum, as we were halfway down the road. Oh no! We returned to get it, and then raced on to school.

Here I am with my class. We are lining up, ready to go into school.

I hurried straight to class. After assembly, we went outside to the playground for our jump-rope lesson. It really wakes you up!

This is my teacher, Mrs. Ridings.

Serious stuff

My school is in New South Wales, which is a state in Australia. Each state creates its own school syllabus (the list of subjects we study) and exams.

Back in the classroom, we had to present our Earth Day project for news time—a show-and-tell lesson. We'd all brought a native plant of Australia to show the class. My friend Jordan and I talked about different species of spinifex grass and how you can use them to purify water, make glue, start a fire, and even build a roof!

Mrs. Ridings then asked us to write a poem about our plant.

Spinifex

Grips the dunes, holds the sands,
slows the wind, hugs the land.
Dry blades make my campfire light,
spread sparks into the deep, dark night,
and afterwards, as the ashes lie,
green shoots rise up toward the sky.
Its roots like hands, the ground they hold,
these spiky tufts that look like gold.

I didn't have time to finish my poem. It was my turn to use the math program on the computer.

At lunchtime, Jordan and I ate our Vegemite sandwiches and a piece of fruit under the huge, shady tree.

During book-share time, I read *Shirtfront.* It's about Australian-rules football. It's a really ace read.

Art was the last class of the day. We've been making a huge outdoor clock.

— *This is our clock design.*

We're decorating each section of the clock with a different theme. Today, we stenciled stars onto the night-sky section and finished the handprint section. It looked impressive!

After school, I biked to Jordan's house to celebrate getting through our spinifex presentation. All the best. —Solomon ❖

 # Riku in Japan

It was 7:40 a.m. I straightened my sweatshirt and clattered down the stairway of my apartment building to meet my friends waiting outside.

Once we were at school, we took off our outdoor shoes and put on our school sneakers. We put our shoes neatly in our cubbies before walking to our classrooms.

It was Misaki's turn to hold the morning meeting. She told us which areas we had to clean after lunch.

Our first class was Kanji—not my best subject. I tried to look excited as I got out my paper, pens, and pots of ink. I slowly used the nib to make an elegant Japanese character. Hmm. Not bad!

Safety first!

Our fall term starts on September 1st. On the first day of the term, all students in Japan practice safety and earthquake drills.

Thank goodness it was time for math next. I'm like lightning on my soroban! The click-clack of the soroban beads as we worked out the answers was like a really loud orchestra. But soon the only sound was the rustle of paper as we made birds during our origami lesson.

Once we were done we still had time to play roshambo. You don't know roshambo? It's like rock, paper, scissors—but we use our feet as well as our hands. You have to be very quick!

At lunchtime, monitors carefully carried huge pans of rice, fish, and spiced vegetables into the classroom. We ate our lunch  at our desks as usual. Then we changed into our P.E. clothes before going to the gym to clean the wooden floor.

Then we went outside for P.E.
We're putting on a fitness show soon,
so we practiced our jump-rope routine.
I think my team's routine is the best!

Finally! It was time for environmental
studies and our Earth Day project.
We had to present a plan for an
environmentally friendly city of the
future. My group showed our class three
photos. Mine's the one in the middle.

Kendo

Martial arts classes are popular in Japan. Kendo, or sword fighting, is practiced with bamboo swords and protective armor.

"In our city," I explained, "we'll plant beautiful gardens on top of skyscrapers. It will bring birds and beauty to the urban environment."

"That's a great idea!" cried Mr. Kento. So now I feel like I'm on top of the world. —Riku ❖

17

Rupa in India

I don't go to school every day.
Sometimes Mom goes off to work at the
farm, and I have to stay home and help
with the housework. But today, Mom
said I only needed to bring in
the water. Phew!

I walked to
the village school
with my friends.

Then, I changed into my best clothes because I was going to present our Earth Day project to the head ranger of the wetland sanctuary. Mom wanted me to look my best for the photos.

Computers for all

In some rural villages in India, computers have been set up outside local buildings. These computers help us explore and learn together.

But I had to concentrate on math first. We started off with multiplication on the blackboard. We worked together to complete a multiplication table and then we used the table as a design for an embroidery pattern.

Mr. Manu handed out our writing-exercise books next. Today, we practiced Hindi, although we often write in Telugu [TEL-uh-goo]. That's my first language.

Next, we prepared the classroom for our puppet show. We'd made the hand puppets in our art-and-design class and we'd written the play, too. We performed it in English for a class of younger children. They clapped for a long time when the show was over!

Traditional Indian hand puppets

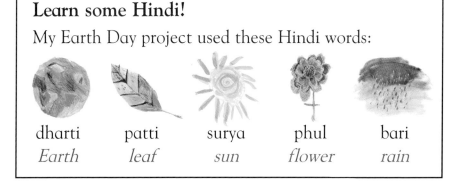

Learn some Hindi!
My Earth Day project used these Hindi words:

dharti	patti	surya	phul	bari
Earth	*leaf*	*sun*	*flower*	*rain*

Next, we ate our lunches in the courtyard. We had rice, hot vegetable curry, and dhal, which is made from spiced peas.

Afterwards, the others played a game called kabbadi. I didn't play because I didn't want to get my clothes dirty.

"Rajesh! Back! Back! Look out for Meena," I squealed. You can't imagine the noise when we play kabbadi! We always sweep up after lunch— but my clothes got me out of it today!

Then my heart began to thump. Mr. Manu introduced us to Mr. Khanna from the wetland sanctuary. We showed

him our Earth Day project. We had identified bog plants that could be used in medicines. It's part of a huge project here in our state, Andhra Pradesh. Mr. Khanna said we'd done a great job, and I smiled for the rest of the day! —Rupa ❖

Fun and games

We don't need equipment for many of our games. To win kabbadi, teams have to take over the other team's territory without getting tagged.

Aseye in Ghana

Hello out there! It's me, Aseye!
I started the day with my gorgeous

chickens. I always give them
their feed of millet seeds
and spinach stalks. Then I
smoothed down my uniform
and dashed to the school
bus. My bag was like a lead
weight with all the books
and school supplies. Mom
works hard at her market
stall to pay for
everything.

We bumped along the damp red earth road, then turned onto the busy highway. Soon, we pulled up at the school—a small building, shaded by fiery-red flame trees and blue jacarandas.

When the bell clanged, we all lined up and filed quietly past another group of students, who were sweeping the verandah with long twig-brooms.

Mrs. Offei was already inside. She smiled broadly. "I know why you're all so restless. It's Earth Day! But math always comes first!"

Mrs. Offei wrote some number sequences on the blackboard. Then we did some number-line problems in our workbooks. We ended with a number-sequence clapping game, which was really fun!

The English spelling test that came next wasn't fun at all. But the spelling bee was an exciting way to end the morning.

We lined up outside for lunch and filled our plates with vegetables, fufu, peanut stew with spinach, and fried fish. Then we made a lot of noise playing a game of ampe.

Play our game!

In ampe, points are based on which legs touch after the players jump. If left touches right, player one scores. If left touches left or right touches right, player two scores.

Our afternoon class was visual arts. We're designing and painting a mural for the red-plaster walls of our new computer room.

Finally, it was Earth Day time. We greeted Mrs. Ampiah from the wildlife park with songs and a dance, which is our custom. We'd practiced hard in our performing-arts class.

Then Mrs. Ampiah announced the winner of the Earth Day prize. Last week, she'd asked us to find ways to protect the young saplings that we were planting in the school yard. Naaku, Yena, and I used some tall collars of tin we'd made in metalwork class. We couldn't believe it when Mrs. Ampiah said we'd found the best solution. We won pencil cases full of school supplies. What a day it's been! —Aseye ❖

Francis in England

After I was woken up by the dustbin lorry (garbage truck), I pulled on my uniform and dashed downstairs for breakfast.

I met Harry on my walk to school. The bell was ringing so we hurried into class for registration. In assembly, we learned about the symbols on the United Kingdom's flag. Did you know England is just one part of the United Kingdom? The others are Scotland, Wales, and Northern Ireland.

Math began with some multiplication and division exercises. Then Mr. Brady outlined our next assignment on the whiteboard. We had to collect information to prove whether most children in the class with blond hair also had blue eyes. Our Venn diagram showed that it was true!

Serious stuff

There are about 3,800 primary schools in England. We're very lucky because school is free. Only five percent of parents choose to pay for a private school.

After a break, Mr. Brady gave us a sports headline from a newspaper and we had to perform a skit showing what the story might be about.

"Compose yourself, take a deep breath, and play to your audience," Mr. Brady reminded us.

Compose ourselves? You should have felt the buzz!

A handwriting lesson was perfect for calming us down before lunch.

We ate lunch in the dining hall, which had been painted by some of my classmates' parents. It's really bright and colorful.

When we were done, we played a game of football (soccer). The game always takes over the playground, but our school has a great climbing frame, too.

Games galore

We often play tag and ball games. In bad weather, we go into the gym and play short tennis, kwik cricket, and basketball.

This afternoon we continued to work on our citizenship project about birds and trees. In the computer room, we researched what birds we might see in the school yard. Earlier this month, we'd built birdhouses and today we finally added the finishing touches. We then all went out to the school yard to put them up in the trees.

We all cheered for Earth Day when our birdhouses were in place.

After school, I played cricket with my dad in the garden (backyard) and then practiced playing my guitar for a bit. My chords don't screech as much as they used to! See ya! —Francis

❖

Samantha in the United States

This morning, I was in the school-bus line early for a change! I was really excited. It was my turn to raise our school's American flag with Principal McGovern.

Afterwards, I rejoined my class to say the Pledge of Allegiance. During the pledge, we place our hands on our hearts while facing the flag.

It kind of helps us all pull together for the day.

We started class with a reading of *Flat Stanley*. In the story, after Stanley is flattened, he's mailed to a different state to visit a friend. (More on that later!) Then we did a spelling assignment based on the story.

State education

There are about 38 million elementary-school children in the United States. Each state has its own guidelines on education.

Then it was time for math. (Hey! We all do math in the morning!) I had to explain my long division answer in front of the whole class. It took forever!

In science, we figured out how healthy our lunches were. My turkey sandwich on whole wheat had lots of protein and vitamins in it! I felt healthy eating it for lunch.

At recess, Cherise and I monkeyed around on the jungle gym in the playground.

I loved our scratch-art class. We'd already painted over the colored layer on our scratchboards. So, I carefully used the pointed wooden stick to scratch away the black paint. The colors underneath made a really awesome contrast!

Samantha Cutrona

My Flat Stanley

Then we talked about our Earth Day projects. At the beginning of the year, we each made a Flat Stanley (remember him?) that could be mailed from friend to friend like in the story. Mine's been all over the world since I first mailed him to Francis. Each friend sent me postcards and notes about their homes. They made my report really special.

My last class was music. I played the recorder. My mouth felt dry and funny afterwards.

After school, it was time for my softball game—and guess what? Our team won! Bye bye for now. —Samantha ❖

Long days—long vacations!
We are at school for about seven or eight hours every day. But we get two and a half months of summer vacation from June to August.

Frida in Peru

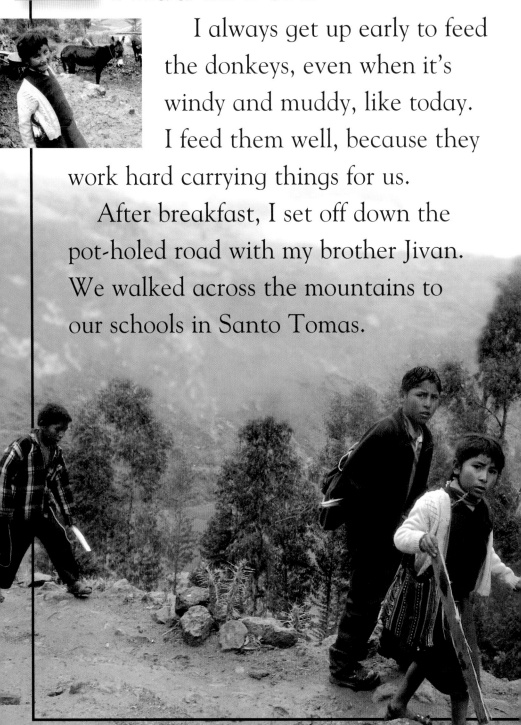

I always get up early to feed the donkeys, even when it's windy and muddy, like today. I feed them well, because they work hard carrying things for us.

After breakfast, I set off down the pot-holed road with my brother Jivan. We walked across the mountains to our schools in Santo Tomas.

The noisy buzzing in my classroom soon fizzled out as Mrs. Tola began our communication lesson. We wrote poems in our language, Quechua [KECH-uh-wuh]. My poem was all about the natural world around us.

Here's my poem in English.

Home

Wind calls the Andes
like a flute's shrill.
Could I ask for more?

Condor swoops above me
weaving his thrills.
Could I ask for more?

Llama keens his eyes
guarding cold hills.
Could I ask for more?

Mama stokes the stove,
stirs the pot, holds me still.
I ask no more.

My language

You might know some Quechua words, such as condor, puma, and llama. I speak Southern Quechua, which has a very rich tradition of storytelling, poetry, and music.

Mrs. Tola chose my poem for our wall display. Everyone made a picture based on the words. I drew the Andes mountains.

"How can we paint the wind?" asked Paulo.

"We dance the movement of wind, don't we? So we can paint it, too," said Mrs. Tola, as she set out some graph paper for math.

We had to design a two-tiered chocolate box and then work out how many different chocolate shapes would fit into the space.

Lunch was a warming meal of quinoa [KEEN-wah] with chili-flavored meat and vegetable stew.

Quinoa

"Let's eat quickly," I said to Carolina, "or there won't be time to play marbles before story time."

Marbles

Llamas on the lookout

Some Quechua people keep llamas on the hillsides to guard their sheep from small predators. Llamas are also used to carry loads, and their fur makes excellent wool for clothes.

After school, Jivan took me to the computer room at his secondary school so I could write an e-mail. The room is paid for by the government.

This afternoon, we'll join our village on the Earth Day work-in. We're building fences around the young trees that we planted on our hillsides last month. The llamas were chewing them all to pieces!

And now I'm going to salute you all with a glass of refreshing yellow Inca Cola! Cheers! —Frida ❖

Glossary

Andes
A range of mountains along the west coast of South America.

Andhra Pradesh
The fourth-largest state in India. India is divided into 29 states.

Assembly
A time when the whole school or a group of classes gathers together.

Blackboard
A board painted black, which is written on with chalk.

Citizenship project
A project that teaches you what it means to be a good citizen.

Communication
A class about reading, writing, listening, and speaking.

Cubby
A small space used for storage.

Elementary school or primary school
A school for younger children, sometimes including kindergarten.

Fufu
An African food made from boiling flour or starchy vegetables in water.

Graph paper
Paper with fine grid lines for plotting diagrams.

High school or secondary school
A school for older children, who have finished elementary school.

Hindi
The national language of India.

Kanji
The Chinese-based characters of the modern Japanese writing system.

Kwik cricket or kanga cricket
A fast-paced ball-and-bat game for children.

Metalwork
A class about shaping metals to make useful things.

Performing arts
A dance, movement, and drama class.

Pledge of Allegiance
A promise to serve your country.

Quinoa
The grainlike fruit of an herb grown in the Andes.

Spelling bee
A spelling competition.

Visual arts
An art class that includes painting, sculpture, film, and photography.

Wetland sanctuary
An area of marshland set aside to protect plants and wildlife.

Whiteboard
A large touch screen linked to a computer.

Index